101 Fast Funny Food Jokes

by PHIL HIRSCH

illustrated by Don Orehek

SCHOLASTIC INC.
New York Toronto London Auckland Sydney

ISBN 0-590-32421-7

Published by Scholastic Inc.

12 11 10 9 8 7 7/8

Printed in the U.S.A. 01

To LAURA
Burger King has the Whopper,
but we have the Bopper!
and
to MARC
McDonald's has its Mac,
but we have our Marc!

THIS WAY TO FOOD JOKES

YOU DESERVE A JOKE TODAY!

How do they prevent crime at McDonald's?

With a burger alarm!

How did Ronald McDonald celebrate his engagement to Wendy?

He gave her an onion ring!

Wendy's
McDonald's

What happens to an enraged 14-foot monster who charges into Burger King?

He has it his way!

What did Ali Baba order at McDonald's?

Two all-beef patties on an "open sesame" seed bun!

FINGER LICKIN' GOOD!

How can you recognize a vampire in a chicken store?

He's the one with the cape-on!

How can you tell that Superman loves chicken?

His real name is Cluck Kent!

Why did the man put suntan lotion on his chicken?

He liked dark meat!

Where do chickens love to vacation?

In the state of Hennessee!

BARBECUED RIB TICKLERS

How does a hungry man eat a hot dog?

With relish!

How does a hungry ghost eat a hot dog?

By goblin' it!

Which famous poet invented French fries?

Edgar Allan Poe-tato!

Why are burgers fast food favorites in Hollywood?

They get all the meaty rolls (roles)!

FOODLAND'S TOP TV SHOWS

I Love Juicy

F(l)ame

Mag-yum yum P.I.

Entertain-mint Tonight

Starchy and Hutch

*M*A*S*H Potatoes*

That's Inedible!

Pork and Mindy

The Fats of Life

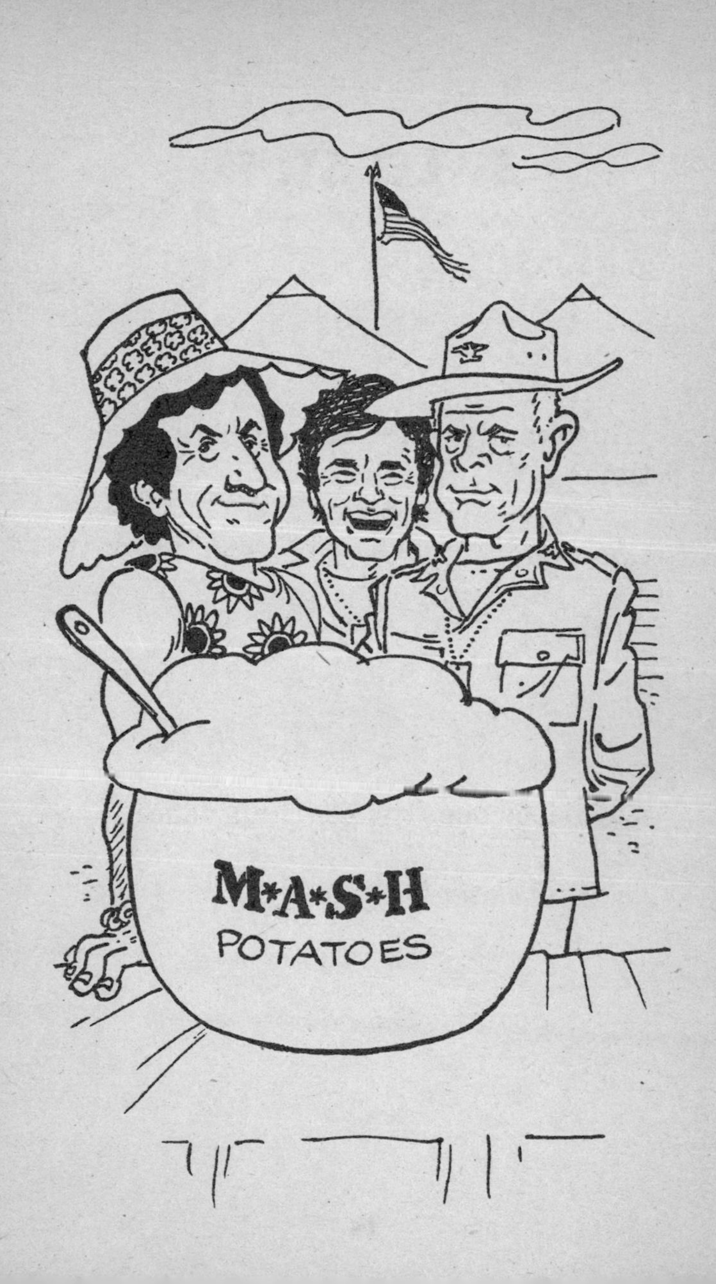
M*A*S*H
POTATOES

SWEET STUFF

Which candy can't get anywhere on time?

Choco-late!

Which food does the best hula dance?

The milk shake!

How do you make a raspberry swirl?

Send it to ballet school!

What food can never become heavyweight champion of the world?

The lollipop – it always gets licked!

EXIT

BERRY DELICIOUS JOKES

What is the best way to raise strawberries?

With a spoon!

What do we know about the insides of cherries?

They're the pits!

What fruit is on a nickel?

A date!

Why wouldn't the lemon help the orange?

It could sour their friendship!

WHY? WHY? WHY?

Why did the jelly roll?

It saw the apple turn over!

Why did the audience throw eggs at the actor?

Because ham and eggs go well together!

Why did the doughnut shop close?

The owner got tired of the (w)hole business!

Why did the young man go into the pizza business?

He wanted to make some dough!

PIZZA
BAKER

Why does everybody like to get together at the local hamburger joint?

It's a perfect meating place!

Why wouldn't you buy a used car from a fresh fruit dealer?

You might end up with a lemon!

DINING OUT

Diner: I'm so hungry I could eat a horse.

Waitress: Then you certainly came to the right place!

Diner: How do you say eat in French?

Waitress: Eat in French!

Diner: Waiter, what's this fly doing in my soup?

Waiter: Looks like the backstroke, sir!

FOODLAND'S MUSIC GROUPS & STARS

The Grapeful Dead

The Peach Boys

Hall and Oatesmeal

Chopstyx

Berry Manilow

Jackson Brownie

The Bean Gees

Fleetwood Macintosh

Bread Zeppelin

FAST FOOD FAVORITES

What did the famous Indian fighter call his fast food ice cream chain?

Custard's Last Stand!

Why did McDonald's get angry at the new fast food chain?

Their slogan was, "You deserve a steak today"!

What was the royal scandal in Fast Foodland?

When Dairy Queen left Burger King for Sir Loin!

What do they call it when two seeded bagels at Bagel Nosh decide to go steady?

Poppy love!

Would octopus make a good fast food?

You must be squidding!

JOKES BY THE BUNCH

What are the best days of the week in Foodland?

Fry-day and Sundae!

What other days are appreciated?

Munchday, Chewsday, and Thirstday!

What happened at the hamburger joint when the workers went on strike?

Things came to a grinding halt!

What happened to the race car driver who went on a diet?

He cracked up – it was a "crash" diet!

FAST FOODLAND'S CELEBRITY PARADE

Which famous mystery writer is named after a Kentucky Fried Chicken recipe?

Agatha Crispy!

Which great comedian would make a terrible cook?

George Burns, of course!

Which famous president do hot dogs love best?

Frank-lin D. Rolls-evelt!

VOTE

If Hungarians eat goulash and Mexicans eat tacos, what do Chinese eat?

Chow Mein-ly!

If spinach makes Popeye strong, what makes him romantic?

Olive Oyl, of course!

If potatoes have eyes and corn has ears, what do peas have?

Each other!

If fruit comes from a fruit tree, what kind of tree does a chicken come from?

A poul-tree!

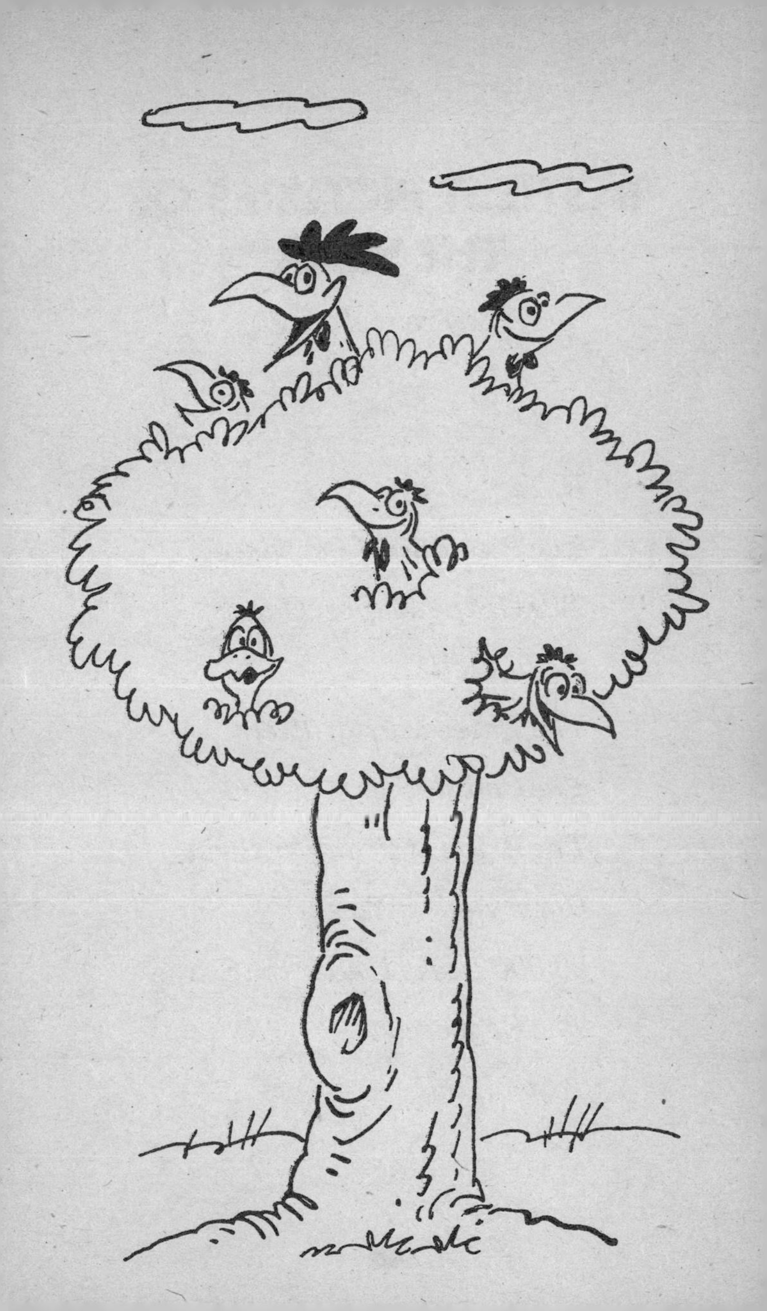

TASTIEST PICTURES OF THE YEAR

(They're *reel* good!)

E. Tea.

The Pie-rates of Penzance

The Grape Muppet Caper

Hello, Deli!

The Three Mustardteers

The Cod Father

The Bride of Frank 'n' Stein

Cherry-ots of Fire

20,000 Leeks Under the Sea

The Eggsorcist

Tootsie Roll

MONSTROUSLY FUNNY FOOD JOKES

When does Dracula find time to eat?

During a coffin break!

What is the vampire's favorite dish?

Ghoulash!

What is the vampire's favorite snack?

Neck-tarines!

Why don't vampires eat sirloins and T-bones?

Because they keep away from stakes!

PUN TIME

Why do all nuts love Shakespeare?

Because he wrote, "To be or nut to be..."!

Why do so many meats have good manners?

Because they are braised properly!

Why did the Triscuit lock itself in the bank vault?

So it could become a safe-cracker!

What game do rural cops enjoy?

Crops and robbers!

Where do you park a truckload of pigs?

In an empty porking place!

WHAT? WHAT? WHAT?

What kind of bar doesn't serve drinks?

A chocolate bar!

What kinds of jokes do vegetables like best?

Corny ones!

What kind of food is crazy about money?

A dough-nut!

What can you say about Frank Perdue and Colonel Sanders?

They're for the birds!

What has a thousand ears but can't hear?

A cornfield!

FOODLAND'S TOP TEN MOVIE STARS

Cheryl Lard

Rabbit Redford

Goldie Hen

Lauren Bagel

Barbra Streisandwich

Vincent Slice

Jane Fondue

Ingrid Burgerman

Pea Marvin

Beet Midler

FAT AND JUICY JOKES

Where do most outstanding hamburgers end up?

In the Hall of Flame!

What did the hamburger say to the pickle?

You're dill-icious!

Where do burgers like to dance ?

At a meat ball!

Why did the chopped meat get slapped in the face?

It was fresh!

DISH UP THE LAUGHS!

Where are the best tacos served?

In the Gulp of Mexico!

What did the hungry astronaut see?

An Unidentified Frying Object!

What did the preacher say at the pickle wedding?

"Dilly Beloved, we are gathered here together..."!

FAMOUS FOODLAND EXPRESSIONS

Stew unto others...

Let's berry the hatchet...

A starch in time saves nine...

Give me liver-ty or give me death...

Tacos cheap...

Early to bread, early to rise...

HOW? HOW? HOW?

How did they honor John Q. Rye when he was named "Breadwinner of the Year"?

They toasted him!

How is Humpty-Dumpty best described?

As "one good egg"!

How is celery born?

The "stalk" brings it!

How come the hot dog was shivering?

It was served with chili beans!

FOODLAND'S TOP BANANAS — Favorite Comics of All Time

Peter Fork

Bread Buttons

Joan Livers

David Steinburger

Lico-Rich Little

Phyllis Dill-Pickle

Bean Martin and Cherry Lewis

MORE FAST FOOD FAVORITES

Where did Superman open his fast food restaurant?

Somewhere near Lois Lane!

Which drink do fast food customers cheer for the most?

Root beer!

Where do they hold prizefights in Fast Foodland?

In an onion ring!

Why did the man climb to the roof of the fast food restaurant?

They told him the meal was on the house!

PHIL'S
FAST FOOD
RESTAURANT

Why would fast food lovers do well in marathons?

Those people like to eat and run!

JUST FOR LAUGHS!

What has lots of teeth but can't chew?

A comb!

What foods stick together?

Staple foods!

What do you call a cat who eats a lemon?

A sourpuss!

What do you call a cat who eats a pickle?

A pickle puss!

SUNKIST

WHO'S WHO IN FOODLAND

Who was the most fruitful conqueror of all time?

Alexander the Grape!

And which conqueror do all bakers like best?

Attila the Bun!

Which movie actress really takes the cake?

Doris Day-nish!

Who is Foodland's favorite cartoon character?

Duck Tracy, of course!

WELL-SEASONED JOKES

Why are chefs hard to like?

Because they beat eggs, whip cream, and mash potatoes!

How would you serve lion meat at a restaurant?

As a mane dish!

Who cornered the spice market?

Herb, of course!

When is it okay to serve milk in a saucer?

Only when you're serving a cat!

WHICH? WHICH? WHICH?

Which foods are especially good for young people?

The pro-teens!

Which Shakespearean play is about food?

"Taming of the Stew"!

Which foods get to go to the best colleges?

The Grade A foods!

Which food is essential to good music?

The beet!

QUICKIE QUIZ

Can you name all these food lovers from *The Wizard of Oz*?

1.

1. *The Munch-kins.*

2. *Auntie Em (& M).*

3.

3. The Wicked Sand-witch of the West.

4.

4. *The Straw(berry) Man.*

5.

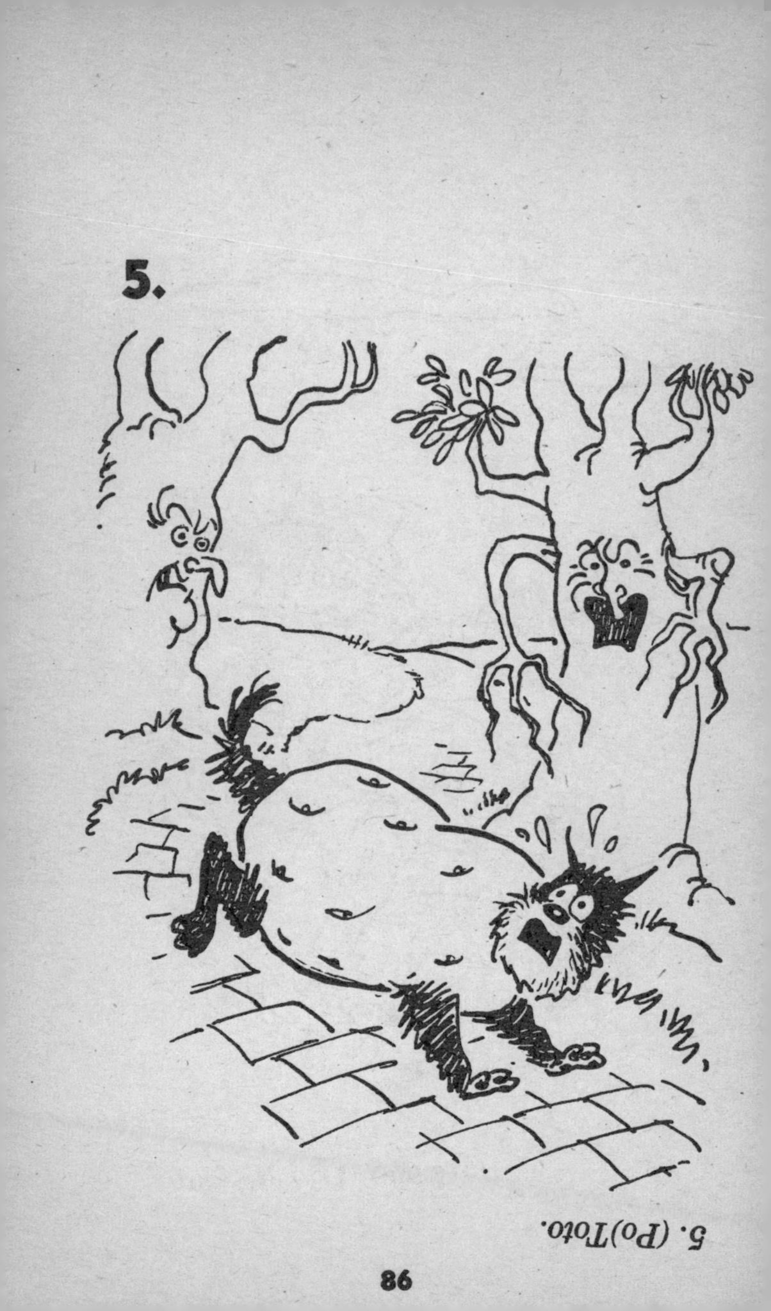

5. (Po)Toto.

FOODLAND'S FAVORITE SONGS

Yankee Noodle Dandy

It Had to be Stew

Of Tea I Sing

Roe, Roe, Roe Your Boat

Fry Me to the Moon

There's No Business Like Dough Business

FRESH PICKED PUNS

Which vegetable shouldn't be allowed to fight in Madison Square Garden?

Spinach—it can get creamed!

Which vegetables can you buy in jewelry stores?

Carats, of course!

Which vegetables can't be trusted with state secrets?

Leeks!

HOW? HOW? HOW?

How can you turn a tomato into squash?

Throw it up in the air—it will come down SQUASH!

How do most lawyers buy food?

By the case!

How do you learn to eat spaghetti?

By using your noodle!

How do vegetables trace their ancestry?

They go back to their roots!

How does celery celebrate Christmas?

It hangs up its stalking!

ODDS 'N' ENDS

Where does a pickle love to eat?

In a dilly-catessen!

Where do cauliflowers love to vacation?

Caulifornia!

Where do gangster chickens live?

Chickago!

What do you think of this book?

Eggs-ellent!